A Family in Singapore

LIBRARY OF CONGRESS CATALOGING-IN-PUBLICATION DATA

Goom, Bridget.
  A family in Singapore.

  Previously published as: Singapore family. © 1984.
  Summary: Text and pictures present the life of twelve-
year-old Chor Ling and her family, residents of a town in
Singapore.
  1. Singapore—Social life and customs—Juvenile literature.
[1. Singapore—Social life and customs]
I. Mathews, Jenny, ill. II. Title.
DS598.S74G66   1986   959.6'705   86-2
ISBN 0-8225-1663-2 (lib. bdg.)

Manufactured in the United States of America

1 2 3 4 5 6 7 8 9 10 96 95 94 93 92 91 90 89 88 87 86

A Family in Singapore

Bridget Goom
Photographs by Jenny Mathews

Lerner Publications Company • Minneapolis

Chor Ling is 12 years old. She lives in the town of Ang Mo Kio in Singapore, a small country between Malaysia and Indonesia.

She is wearing her school uniform. It's hot all year in Singapore, so she never needs to wear a coat. But it rains a lot, especially in November and December. She often needs an umbrella.

M A L A Y S I

Juron

I N D I A

Indian Ocea

4

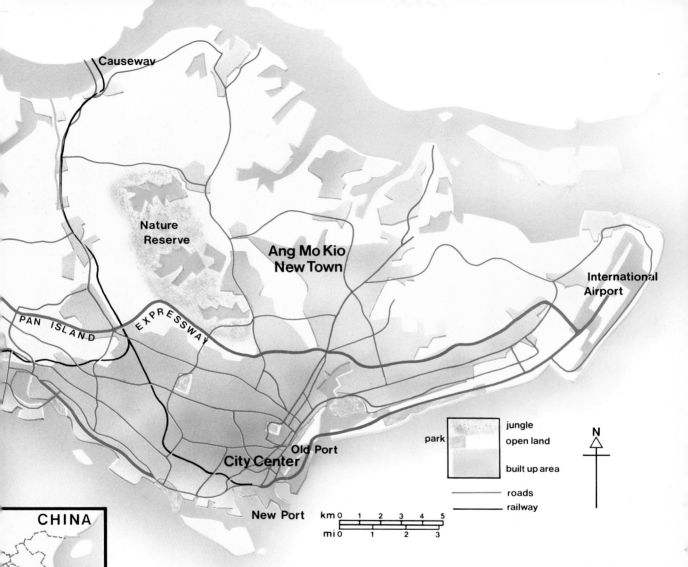

Chor Ling lives with her parents and her little brother, Chor Sen. Their apartment is on the sixth floor of a big tower building. They moved there six years ago when the building had just been built. Everyone in Chor Ling's town lives in an apartment and all the buildings are new. Chor Ling's mother likes their apartment because it is modern and easy to clean.

5

Like everyone else in their building, Chor Ling's mother hangs the family's wash on long poles outside their window to dry. She has had a lot of practice and never drops anything.

Chor Ling's mother shops at a market very near their apartment. The market is open every day but the busiest day is Sunday.

Chor Ling's mother buys all their fruit at the market. Many different kinds of fruit are available, but none are grown in Singapore. The country is very small and most of the land is used for buildings. Not much room is left for farming.

Some of the fruit comes from Malaysia. Trucks full of watermelons, pineapples, mangoes and coconuts cross the border into Singapore every day. Other kinds of fruit come from countries like Australia, China and America.

Chor Ling's mother buys vegetables, meat, fish and tofu (bean curd) at the market, as well as fruit. Tofu is made from soybeans. It looks and tastes a little like plain yogurt, and it can be cooked many different ways.

Soy milk is also made from soybeans, and Chor Ling thinks it is delicious. Her mother often stops to have a glass while she is shopping. It is very good for you because soybeans are full of protein.

Chor Ling helps her mother shop in the market. They eat rice or noodles almost every day, but they don't often eat bread or potatoes. They can buy plain white noodles, yellow egg noodles, or dried noodles at the market. Chor Ling's mother prefers fresh noodles.

Chor Ling's mother babysits for a little boy who doesn't go to school yet. His parents sell fish in the market, and they bring him to Chor Ling's apartment on their way to work. His mother picks him up in the afternoon.

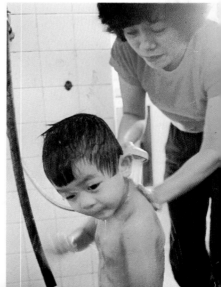

One of Chor Ling's school friends has come over for lunch. Chor Ling's mother has fixed prawns, fish, vegetables, rice and soup. The red sauce in the small dishes is made with chilies and is very hot and spicy.

Chor Ling's father eats with chopsticks. He says his food doesn't taste right when he eats with a fork and spoon.

At home, Chor Ling's family speaks a Chinese language called Teochew. But she and Chor Sen speak English for most of their lessons at school. They are also learning another Chinese language called Mandarin.

Chor Ling is in her last year in primary school. She has to work very hard because if she doesn't pass the exams at the end of the year she won't be able to go on to secondary school. She has extra lessons in mathematics and Mandarin and does a lot of homework every night.

There are forty-five children in Chor Ling's class at school. As in most schools in Singapore, there isn't room for all the children to have lessons at the same time. Chor Ling has school in the afternoon, and a different class has lessons in the morning.

Chor Ling and Chor Sen catch the school bus at 11:45 A.M. and school starts at 12:45 P.M. They have lessons until 3:00, when they stop for a snack, usually fried noodles. After the break, they have class until six o'clock, when it's time to go home.

One of the things Chor Ling likes best about school is the library. She often borrows books to read. She can read English and Chinese, but she likes the English stories best.

Chor Ling doesn't spend all her time reading, however. Her whole family goes to the big swimming pool near their apartment once or twice a week. Chor Ling is a very good swimmer. Her brother learned to swim about three years ago. Chor Sen is getting faster all the time, but Chor Ling can still beat him in races.

Next to the pool is a snack bar. Chor Sen always has a big plate of noodles after he's been swimming.

Chor Ling's father likes to swim, too, but he never goes to the pool on weekends. He drives a taxi and his busiest day is Sunday.

He drives all over Singapore in his taxi. When he goes out near the port, he can watch the ships being loaded with goods.

In the new part of the port, all the goods are moved around in big boxes called containers. The containers are moved off the ship by huge cranes and loaded onto trucks. About two thousand containers can be moved in an hour and it doesn't take long to load or unload a ship this way.

In the old part of the port, they don't use containers. Many more people work in this part of the port, but it still takes a long time to load and unload the ships.

The new port is soon going to be made much bigger. Some buildings near the port will be torn down to make room. When the work is finished, Singapore will be the biggest port in the world. It's already second biggest, after Rotterdam in Holland.

Chor Ling's father used to drive a bus, but he likes driving a taxi better. It gives him more time to talk to people. He speaks three Chinese languages: Teochew, Hokkien and Mandarin. He also knows Malay and English. This is very useful, since so many languages are spoken in Singapore.

Many signs are written in more than one language so everyone can read them. The "Danger" sign below is written in English, Chinese, Tamil and Malay.

There are other Chinese languages in addition to the ones Chor Ling's father speaks. Although they all sound quite different, the languages are written the same way.

In Teochew, "Warning, Danger" sounds like this:

ngui   hiam

In Mandarin, "Warning, Danger" sounds like this:

wei   xian

But they are both written like this:

All the people who speak different Chinese languages can read the same Chinese newspapers, books, and signs.

When Chor Ling's father isn't working, he likes to play chess with his friends. They have a chess table set up where it's shady and cool, and play every day.

They play Chinese chess, not international chess. The board is a little different and the pieces go where the lines cross, instead of in the squares. Chess is a very old game which was first played in India.

Chor Sen can't play chess yet, but he likes to play *caroms*. His aunt gave him a board for his birthday. In caroms, you try to knock the pieces into the holes at the corners of the board by hitting them with a piece called the striker. Most of Chor Ling's and Chor Sen's friends play caroms. It is very popular in Singapore and Malaysia.

On weekends and during school vacation, Chor Ling often visits her grandmother. Grandmother lives in a house in a *kampong*, which is a kind of village. Chor Ling loves going there because it's so friendly.

When Chor Ling was small, her family lived in the kampong too. They moved to their apartment when Chor Ling was six.

The houses in the kampong are made of wood. Some have metal roofs and some have thatch on top of the metal to keep the houses cool. All of the houses are much older than Chor Ling's apartment building.

Chor Ling's grandmother now has running water, gas to cook on, and electric lights in her house. But when Chor Ling's father was young, all the water for cooking, drinking and washing came from a well outside the house. Grandmother washed clothes in a stream in the middle of the kampong. It was hard work, but she always had someone to talk to.

When Chor Sen plays near the stream, he sometimes falls down and gets covered in mud. His grandmother helps him clean up before his mother finds out.

Chor Ling's grandmother won't live in the kampong much longer. The government says that the kampong land is needed for new high-rise buildings. Grandmother and her neighbors will all have to move and their wooden houses will be knocked down to make room for big blocks of apartments and factories.

Grandmother puts some of the plants from her garden in pots to take with her to her new apartment.

Grandmother has lots of photographs of her house and family. When she shows Chor Ling and Chor Sen her photograph album, she tells them stories about when she was a child.

She was born in China and brought to Singapore when she was a baby. She doesn't remember China or the trip across the sea, but she remembers her parents telling her about it.

Chor Ling's grandfather was also born in China. Like many other people from China or India, his family came to Singapore to look for work. Malaysian people have lived in Singapore for a long time. Singapore and part of Malaysia were once one country.

Chor Ling's grandfather died a few years ago. Every day, her grandmother lights sticks of incense and puts them by his photograph to honor his memory. Many Chinese also burn incense at home in memory of their ancestors, or in the Chinese temple when they pray.

There are many different religions in Singapore. Some of them are Taoism, Buddhism, Islam, Christianity, and Hinduism. Whenever there is an important religious festival, everyone has a day's vacation.

Chor Ling's favorite holiday is the Mooncake Festival. It is a Taoist festival held in September or October when the moon is full.

At the festival, there are mooncakes to eat. Mooncakes are round like the full moon, made of pastry and filled with good things like red bean paste.

During the festival, puppet shows and stalls are set up in the streets. Chor Sen watches the puppet shows, with their beautiful costumes, over and over.

25

Everyone joins in the festival. The shops are full of colored lanterns made of paper. The lanterns are made in all different shapes, such as fish, birds, or airplanes, and they are lighted by candles inside.

When Chor Ling and her family still lived in the kampong, she thought the festival was very exciting. There weren't many electric lights and the lanterns really showed up in the darkness. In Ang Mo Kio, the street lamps and buildings shed so much light that the lanterns don't make very much difference.

Chor Ling's family is going to the Chinese Gardens in Jurong for the festival this year. The gardens are very dark at night, and there will be thousands of people carrying lanterns.

On the way to the garden, before dark, they might stop at McDonald's for a hamburger. Chor Ling's father teases that it is far too expensive and they won't have room left to eat mooncakes. But Chor Ling knows that everyone does something special at festival time.

27

History of Singapore

People have lived on the island of Singapore for thousands of years. At first, they shared the jungle island with tigers and other wild animals.

Beginning about 1100 A.D., more people moved to the island. Temasek, the first big trading city in Singapore harbor, was destroyed in 1377 by invaders from Indonesia. But pirates and fishing fleets still made Singapore their base. The pirates would set out from there to raid the ships passing nearby.

In 1819, Sir Stamford Raffles of England was looking for a shipping depot. He worked for the East India Company, the biggest English trading company at that time. The company needed a good harbor, close to its major shipping routes, where ships could rest, get repairs, and resupply. Sir Raffles made a deal with the sultan of Johor (now part of Malaysia) for the right to use the harbor of Singapore.

Because of the amount of shipping the East India Company moved through the port, Singapore grew very rapidly in size. People moved there from China, India, and Malaysia to find jobs. In 1824 England gained control of the entire island.

The British built air bases on Singapore in the 1920s and 1930s, to help defend the island in case of war. However, they lost it to Japan overnight in 1942. The British did not regain control until 1945.

Singapore began to gain its independence from Britain after World War II. It has been an independent country since 1965.

Facts about Singapore

Capital: Singapore

Official Languages:
Chinese, English, Malay, Tamil
> English is used in business and government, and is the first language used in most schools.

Form of Money: the Singapore dollar

Area: 238 square miles (616 square kilometers)
> Singapore covers about the same area as the city of Chicago.

Population: about 2,600,000
> About one-tenth as many people live in Singapore as in the United States. Three-fourths of the people in Singapore are of Chinese descent.

NORTH
AMERICA

SOUTH
AMERICA

EUROPE

ASIA

AFRICA

Singapore

AUSTRALIA

Families the World Over

Some children in foreign countries live like you do. Others live very differently. In these books, you can meet children from all over the world. You'll learn about their games and schools, their families and friends, and what it's like to grow up in a faraway land.

A FAMILY IN CHINA	A FAMILY IN PAKISTAN	A FAMILY IN BRAZIL
A FAMILY IN EGYPT	A FAMILY IN SRI LANKA	A FAMILY IN CHILE
A FAMILY IN FRANCE	A FAMILY IN WEST GERMANY	A FAMILY IN IRELAND
A FAMILY IN INDIA	AN ABORIGINAL FAMILY	A FAMILY IN MOROCCO
A FAMILY IN JAMAICA	AN ARAB FAMILY	A FAMILY IN SINGAPORE
A FAMILY IN NIGERIA	AN ESKIMO FAMILY	A ZULU FAMILY

Lerner Publications Company
241 First Avenue North
Minneapolis, Minnesota 55401